Night Swim

new poetry by

Benjamin Gilmour

ISBN: 9798582760153

Also by Benjamin Gilmour:
Song of a Hundred Miles
Cameras & Kalashnikovs
The Travel Bug
Paramedico
The Gap

Author's Note:
Don't read them all at once…

POEMS

<u>Firework</u>

At the band's
    crescendo,
a firework
    blinded you.

Before the flash
    there were dancing
    girls,
faces of children,
    mirrors
    of cosmic dust.

Now you will live
    in this night
    forever.

The night
    of fireflies
    and wonder,
the night
    when stars
    applauded,
the night
    the light
    went out.

Table

I fell in love with a table,
old as my mother,
beautiful as the girl
who brought me
Andalusian
wine.

I counted the rings,
the ripples
of time,
the story of
ninety years,
under my olives.

I fell in love with a table,
and read it's scars
with fingers
that know only
the language of
cigarettes.

Night Reader

Each night her novels
    are heavier,
    thicker,
her tower of books
    a shadow
    on the wall.

Each night her novels
    seduce her
    like a man
with strong hands,
    folding her
    into his pages.

Each night I watch
    the eyes I love
    flick
from line to line,
    like bees at flowers
    I cannot see.

Each night I dream
    of becoming
    her book,
a thriller
    she'll never
    put down.

Devotion

I sleepwalk through the valley
    of your night-skin,
collect the washed-up shells
    of your dreams.

I put them on the balcony
    I've opened for you,
where wind and small birds
    talk about summer.

I wait at the door of your breath
    for the word 'love',
but know that even in your silence,
    your heart never sleeps.

<u>Invitation</u>

Love, you leave
    the hearts
    of men
dark as mountains
    on a map
    of the world.

You're the sailor's suicide,
    the poet's
    broken neck.
You give me tea, but
    your poison
    is sweet.

You are one love,
    and countless
    deaths.
Love, will you
    come with me
    tonight?

The Air She Breathes

I am the air
she breathes,
she said.

Without me
there is no life,
she said.

And still
she lives and breathes,
they said.

The Ghost of Lost Love

The heart has made a sigh,
the ghost of lost love
vented with the moan
of a distant factory.

The sound it rises
over cities, oceans,
mountains, valleys.

The heart has made a sigh,
with no reply,
the ghost
of lost love.

<u>Garden</u>

There are places
in this garden
where fruits ripen,
where insects
give birth,
where parsley
waits.

There are places
in this garden
where small animals
lie in unmarked
graves,
and the earth is ready
for seeds.

There are places
in this garden
where leaves
grow old together,
stalks embrace
in passion,
and buds
hide blushing
faces.

There are places
in this garden
where poetry
is sprouting.

In three weeks

In three weeks
you will be married
to a man
with a ute
who lays concrete over grass,
who can stand atop a ladder
with nails
between his lips
who swears about the weather
with his mates who get together,
in three weeks.

In three weeks
you will be married
to a man
who smells like brick-work,
who you serve with beer and biscuits
who will grunt and fix and lift things,
who will sweat, but
don't you like that?
Won't you like that
in three weeks?

In three weeks
you will be married
to a man
with no adventure,

who passes by a sunrise
and does not say
good morning,
who has never watched a star
long enough
to see it falling,
in three weeks.

In three weeks
you will be married
to a man
who eats bananas
but does not
dream of islands.

In three weeks
you will be married
and I, I will be sitting,
in three weeks I will be sitting
at the fragile bleeding corner
of the heart
you left
behind.

I Bake a Sun

I bake a sun,
it rises quickly,
the crust is golden,
I bake a sun.

I eat it hot,
it tastes like bees,
it tastes like butter,
I eat it hot.

I tell my lover,
she takes a mouthful,
she fills her mouth full,
I tell my lover.

It makes us sleepy,
warm and happy,
I bake a sun,
it makes us sleepy.

On My Lap

The moon has fallen asleep
    on my lap.

She might be the queen
    of dreams
    and lovers,
but in my hands
    she's a cat.

What a beautiful face
    she has!

Stain

A heart that is
broken,

spills love
on your shirt.

Without Realising

I step
on a beetle,

I don't think
about the family.

Bee

Like every
flower
you visit,
I give you
my nectar.

You won't
stay long,
but even briefly
I can
love you.

Mango

Hanging from
the poet's mind,
fruit of the sun!

You have the shape
and volume
of my heart.

I eat you
and I'm
whole again.

Wave

She kicks off
her shoes

and rushes
to greet me

with the gift
of a shell.

<u>Last Words</u>

A rainbow sprouted
from the ocean.

'I'll cut it down!' said
uncle Bob.

'I'll take my axe
and cut it down.'

Then in his boat
he rowed away.

The Dream I Love

Going to bed
with a day
round my neck,

I found you
with a mouth
full of flowers.

Night Swim

The tree I climbed
was hung with tears,
some old, some ripe, some
falling
to the ground.

But from the top
I saw her on high,
splashing
in a galaxy
of stars.

Figment

I fell in love
with a figment.

She was all the perfect
days, all the
beautiful things, all
the kind words.

I went to visit
my figment (when
I didn't know
she was a figment).

'Meet me at the
corner,' she'd said.

When I left the station
I took my plastic bag
and waited at the corner.

'I'll be holding
an umbrella,' she'd
instructed.

At the corner
there was
no-one.

I waited
for a lifetime
before I realised
I loved a figment.

Twilight

In the dandelions
    a little drum
    is playing.

In the yellow sky
    an orchestra
    assembles.

In my tired heart
    your song is
    the sunset.

Wrong Number

A phone
call

for a lonely
man.

Hibiscus

If a lover doesn't
break you off
to wear
behind her ear,

a bird
will hover by
and steal
your heart.

Seahorse

Galloping the fields
    of aquamarine,
in her wake
    cosmic
    phosphorescence.

See her fine figure S?
    The finesse
    of her effortless
    glide?

I touch her and
    a thousand bubbles
rises from her
    glittering
    hide,
singing the song
    only wild horses
    and wild lovers
    know.

North

An arrowhead
　　of birds,
migrates
　　to my heart.

The steady pulse
　　of wings
whispers
　　in my blood.

Look up
　　and see,
the sky is
　　a compass.

Forest

The tribe of
    handsome trees
doesn't care
one way
    or another
if they're noticed.

None have waited
    a hundred years
    for my eyes.
They're comfortable
    in their own
    bark.

Sometimes I think
they're waving at me,
    but I know
    it's just
    the wind.

The Cage

The cage loves
    a bird,
but a bird
    will never
    love it
    back.

What is the
    cage
    without a
    bird?

Empty
    inside.

Seeds

You talk
    fast as a rocket
even the police
    can't interrupt.

You're on the
    first floor.
    The carpet
of twenty stairs
thinned out
    by your
    ups and
    downs.

As you leave
    slowly,
    gently,
your feet scatter
a dozen winged seeds
    on the
    concrete
    landing.

I think
    of all the seeds
that never
    found earth.

Holy Spirit

Descending through
    a power pole,
it set the worker's head
    alight.

It entered by
    a screwdriver,
departed as
    a golden crown.

The man whose Gods
    were truck and dog
has temples
    of sacred ash.

We cut him from
    his hi-vis shroud,
now obsolete
    illumination.

Shiraz

Killing yourself
    drunk
is easier. So
    he bought
    two bottles
of French Shiraz.

Chatea de Marmot...

I know that wine!
Fifty dollars a bottle!

Surely a man
with taste like this
    has kindness for himself
    to live another
    day?

Greek Voices

His mama shells the
    broad beans, crying.

Crying like the cherub
    in her fountain.

Upstairs he lies asleep,
    her angel son.

His soccer T-shirt
    rises and falls.

All night he yelled
    at voices:

'I will not kill her!
    She's my mama!'

Now he quietly wakes
    to make her coffee.

Unconscious

You have fled
    on the wings
    of valium.

Your face on the pillow,
    the sculpture
    of an angel.

Evening Walk

Let's go for an evening walk,
    you said.

The clouds were pink and lovely,
    but the suburb
    below
    a silhouette
    of hell.

In the house you love
    I found a woman
    dead,
    clots in both
    lungs.

At number 23,
    last year,
    the backyard pool
    swallowed
    a boy.

And that garage
    on the corner?
    The tomb
    of a hanging
    man.

Let's go for an evening walk,
   you said.
Okay then,
   I replied.

<u>Wounded Soldier</u>

On a page
    of my heart
I wrote a poem
    in blood.

I left it at the
    cafe table
under my
    empty cup.

Across the street
    I watched
the waitress
    read my wounds.

Sorry, Grant Green

I stopped
playing jazz
when I heard
a bird
performing
on my
balcony.

I saw the
curious moon
appear across
the sea.
It was only three
in the
afternoon.

I stopped
playing jazz,
to an audience
of none.
But every wave
applauded
the bird.

Night Sky

Calling the night sky
    pretty
    cheapens it.

Just one of those stars
    is worth
    a fortune of words.

Arrival

The wind of your
    love
    blew in like a
    train.

It shook the
    lofts
    of white
    gums,

drummed at
    my window
    like a
    battle cry.

The end of the
    world
    won't wait
    for us.

With no hesitation
    I fling my doors
    open
    to you.

<u>Circle</u>

The circle in
    eyes
    and planets

reminds me
    to embrace
    myself.

As the holder
    and the
    held,

the circle
    is love
    complete.

Bohème

My daughter
imagines being
    a little pig
    on a train.

Round and round
goes the train,
    her smile
    with it.

What I would give
to have a mind
    like hers
    again,

where little
pigs and trains
    are all that
    matters.

Butterfly

I asked
    for a poem
and got
    a butterfly.

It stopped on
    my page
with yellow
    wings.

It's petals opened
    and closed,
in the rhythm
    of verse.

Spring gave me
    a poem,
then took it
    away again.

ABOUT THE AUTHOR

Benjamin Gilmour is a writer, filmmaker and poet living in Northern NSW, Australia. His early poetry has been published in Island Magazine, Quadrant, Going Down Swinging, Overland, Meanjin and other literary journals. His first book of poetry was *Song of a Hundred Miles* (Peculiar Press) in 1998. He is the author of five non-fiction books, including *Paramedico* (Harper Collins) and *The Gap* (Penguin Random House). His film *Jirga* was the Australia entry to the Academy Awards Best Foreign Language Film in 2019.

www.benjamingilmour.com